SKIN CANCER

SKIN CANCER

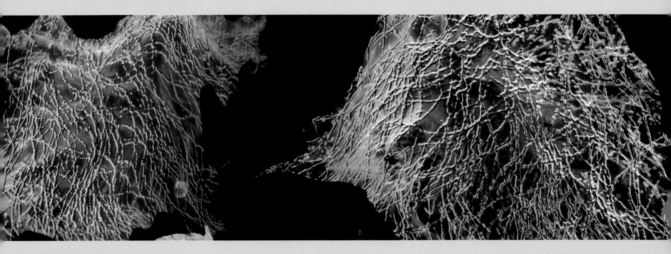

Marjorie L. Buckmaster

 Marshall Cavendish
Benchmark
New York

Marshall Cavendish Benchmark
99 White Plains Road
Tarrytown, New York 10591-9001
www.marshallcavendish.us

This book is not intended for use as a substitute for advice, consultation, or treatment by a licensed medical practitioner. The reader is advised that no action of a medical nature should be taken without consultation with a licensed medical practitioner, including action that may seem to be indicated by the contents of this work, since individual circumstances vary and medical standards, knowledge, and practices change with time. The publisher, author, and medical consultants disclaim all liability and cannot be held responsible for any problems that may arise from use of this book.

Library of Congress Cataloging-in-Publication Data
Buckmaster, Marjorie L.
  Skin cancer / by Marjorie L. Buckmaster.
      p. cm. -- (Health alert)
  Summary: "Discusses skin cancer and its effects on people and society"--Provided by publisher.
  Includes bibliographical references and index.
  ISBN 978-0-7614-2703-2
  1. Skin--Cancer--Juvenile literature. I. Title. II. Series.
  RC280.S5B83 2008
  616.99'477--dc22
                                        2007024623

Front cover: Skin cancer cells

Photo research by Candlepants, Incorporated
Cover credit: Steve Gschmeisnner / Photo Researchers, Inc.

The photographs in this book are used by permission and through the courtesy of:
Photo Researchers: hybrid medical animation, 2; Andrew Syred, 4, 10; Michel Gilles, 9; A.B. Joyce, 21; Hans-Ulrich Osterwalder, 22; Science Source, 27; Mary Evans Picture Library, 30; SPL, 34; Colin Cuthbert, 39; Phanie, 38; David Parker, 45; Mauro Fermariello, 52. Phototake USA: ISM, 16, 42; Nucleus Medical Art, Inc., 13; LookatSciences, 15; Jean Claude Revy, 43; Barry Slaven, MD, PhD, 46; BSIP, 49. Corbis: Jean Michel Foujols/zefa, 24; Bettmann, 32; Naomi Bruzak/epa, 37; Randy Faris, 54. Getty Images: 50.

Printed in China

6 5 4 3 2 1

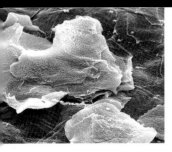

CONTENTS

WHAT IS IT LIKE TO HAVE SKIN CANCER?

For as long as eleven-year-old Sharon could remember, she loved playing outside in the sunshine and swimming in her backyard pool. She and her friends would stay outside all afternoon, hoping to get the kind of tans that they saw on movie stars and models. Sharon and her friends even compared tans to see who would be the first to get darker.

One afternoon when Sharon and her friends were looking at their tans, Sharon noticed a small, dark spot on her arm that had not been there before. She had freckles on her face and body, so she thought that maybe it was a very dark freckle. When she showed the spot to her mother, they agreed that the spot looked unusual. It was darker than her regular freckles and had a weird shape. Sharon and her mother tried to remove it, thinking it was a scab or a piece of something that was stuck to Sharon's skin. But when they did that, the spot started to bleed. Sharon's mom had read about kids developing skin cancer, and wanted a doctor to look at the spot.

Sharon went to a **dermatologist,** a doctor who specializes in skin problems. He examined the spot and ran tests. It turned out that Sharon had a **melanoma,** which is the most dangerous type of skin cancer. The doctor was surprised because melanoma is very rare in children. More often, adults are the ones who develop that form of skin cancer.

In Sharon's case, the melanoma spot was smaller than it would have been on an adult. Adult melanomas are usually about the size of an eraser on the top of the pencil. Because Sharon's melanoma was detected early, the doctor was able to remove the melanoma, and the cancer did not spread to the rest of her body.

Today, Sharon has a small scar on her arm, but it is shrinking as she grows. She also takes better care of her skin by wearing a hat and using **sunblock** or **sunscreen** whenever she spends a lot of time in the sun. Sharon points out her scar to friends who think skin cancer cannot happen to them. She also reminds her friends that frequently using a tanning bed—known among her friends as a "fake baking"—can lead to skin cancer. When asked about her skin cancer, Sharon is not shy about giving people some good advice. "Enjoy the outdoors, but be safe in the sun," she says. "Cover up, wear a hat with a big brim, use a lot of sunblock or sunscreen, do not fake bake in tanning beds, and keep an eye out for any changes in your skin!"

WHAT IS SKIN CANCER?

Different types of cancer can affect different organs or body systems. But among all ages, skin cancer is the most commonly occurring cancer in the United States. Overall, more than 1.3 million skin cancers are diagnosed in each year. That is more than all of the other kinds of cancer combined

As the body's largest organ, the layers of skin are made up of trillions of cells. All living things have cells. These cells work together to carry out all of the functions of life in human beings, plants, animals, and even in the smallest insect. Cells make it possible to throw a ball, eat lunch, study for a test, and walk from one corner of the room to the other—any activity that bodies go through in daily life, including natural activities like breathing and thinking.

Usually, cells reproduce on their own, simply by dividing, or splitting in half to create two identical cells. One cell becomes two, two become four, and so on. The division of normal and healthy cells is what keeps bodies growing, and can sometimes help the body heal itself. For example, cells scraped off a skinned knee are replaced with new cells made from the healthy cells surrounding the cut.

However, some of these functions can only be carried out by normal, healthy cells that continue to divide naturally and normally.

THE SKIN

In order to understand skin cancer and how it develops and affects the body, it is first necessary to explore what the skin is, how it works, and what can go wrong. Since it covers nearly all surfaces of the body, the skin is considered the body's largest organ. Your skin is responsible for protecting your body while also helping you sense the world around you.

Skin Layers

The skin is made up of three main layers-the **epidermis,** the **dermis,** and the **subcutis.** The epidermis is the outermost layer of the skin. The epidermis can be divided into its own

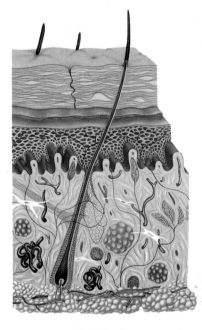

The skin, also called the integumentary system, is made up of several layers. Each layer has a variety of cells that serve different purposes.

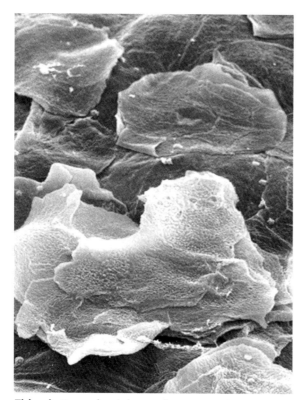

This photograph—taken using a very strong microscope—shows how the outer layers of skin dry up and flake off.

separate layers. The innermost layers have living cells. As some of these cells die and dry up, they move outward to form the outer layer of the epidermis. This horny layer—as it is sometimes called—helps to protect your body from damage. It is like the outer layer of a shield that stops a lot of things from getting inside your body and harming you. Your body is constantly shedding and replacing this outermost layer of dead skin cells.

Melanocytes are located in the epidermis. These are cells that produce **melanin,** which is a substance that gives skin its color. Darker skin has more melanin than lighter skin. Melanin also protects the skin from harmful **ultraviolet** (UV) rays that come from the Sun. Other types of cells can also be found in the inner layers of the epidermis. These include cells that are part of the **immune system,** which protects the body from illness, and sensory cells that help you to sense things in your environment.

The dermis is the second layer of skin. It is the largest portion of the skin, and its thickness helps to protect the body. The dermis is made up of nerves, tissues, blood vessels, and glands. Nerves are a collection of cells that send messages to and from your brain and spinal cord. These messages can be about things you are sensing, like pain, or they can carry orders for your body to follow, such as instructions for certain muscles to move.

Proteins called collagen and elastin can also be found in the dermis. These substances give skin its strength and flexibility. They allow your skin to stretch and move with your body. Blood vessels—and the cells inside and around the vessels—that run through the dermis help the immune system and help bring nutrients to different parts of the body. Sweat glands are one type of gland located in the dermis. Sweating helps your body release extra heat.

The subcutis is the innermost layer of skin. It is mostly made up of fatty cells. These fat cells help to cushion or pad the skin, which helps in protecting your body's muscles and internal organs. Fat cells in this layer help insulate the body, allowing you to maintain a healthy body temperature. Fat cells in the subcutis also store nutrients and food your body needs.

Moles and Other Marks

Melanocytes, blood vessels, and other structures within the skin can cause different marks that you can see. Birthmarks, which are also called hemangiomas, show up early in life. Most birthmarks are caused by a collection of blood vessels in one place. Some birthmarks can be raised, or stick out from the skin. Others are smooth and flat. In most cases, birthmarks are harmless. Some even disappear as a person gets older.

Many people have freckles all over their skin. Freckles are caused by darkened melanocytes. Usually, only people with fair skin and light hair develop freckles. Freckles can become darker or spread when skin is exposed to a lot of Sun. For many people, freckles fade or disappear with age.

Moles are made up of melanocytes that group together and darken. Nearly everybody has moles on some part or many parts of their bodies. They may show up as dark brown, blue, or reddish in color. Moles can stick out from the skin, lie flat, or have hairs growing from them. Most moles are usually round in shape. Sometimes moles can change in shape, size, and color. Some moles will always stay the same.

WHAT GOES WRONG

Cells in the body usually reproduce on their own—most of the time by splitting into more cells. This division of normal and healthy cells is what keeps bodies growing and healing. For example, cells that are lost when a knee is scraped or cut are replaced with new cells made from the healthy cells surrounding the cut.

When a person has skin cancer, their skin cells stop dividing normally. Cancer cells divide in ways that are hard to predict. This can create many irregular groups of cells that pile up into tumors or lesions. Tumors and lesions are names given to groups of cancerous cells. Sometimes cancerous cells can grow and spread to the rest of the body. Other times, they remain localized, or in one area of the body.

Cancer cells interfere with normal body processes. When healthy cells become cancerous, they can no longer perform the jobs that

Cancer cells, shown here in purple, can multiply in the different layers of skin and then spread to other organs.

the body needs them to do. Cancerous cells also harm body processes by taking up space and nutrients that are needed for healthy cells. In serious cases of cancer, cancerous cells multiply uncontrollably and spread to different body systems, eventually causing death.

TYPES OF SKIN CANCER

There are three types of skin cancer. Two types of non-melanoma skin cancer are the kind that are located in one place and are more easily treated by doctors. These types of nonmelanoma skin cancer are called basal cell carcinoma and squamous cell carcinoma. (Carcinoma is another word for cancers that occur on surface tissues.) Malignant melanoma is a more dangerous form of skin cancer because it is the type that spreads to other parts of the body the fastest.

Basal Cell Carcinoma

Basal cell carcinoma accounts for about 80 percent of all skin cancers. It is highly treatable, which means that doctors are usually able to treat the cancer successfully before it spreads and causes a lot of damage. This type of cancer begins at the basal cell level of the skin. These basal cells form a layer in the epidermis.

Basal cell carcinomas grow very slowly. They usually appear as a small, shiny bump on the skin, mostly on those areas that are often exposed to the Sun. This type of skin

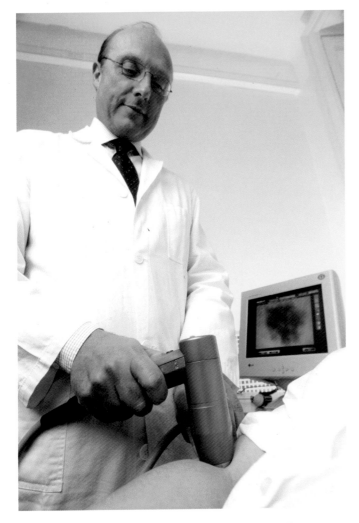

A dermatologist uses a magnifying tool to examine a patient's suspicious mole. Most moles that cause skin cancer are a result of basal cell carcinoma.

cancer is usually found on the head, neck, arms, hands, and face. People most at risk for this kind of cancer usually have light-colored hair and skin.

Squamous Cell Carcinoma

This kind of cancer is the second most common kind of skin cancer. Squamous cell carcinoma usually starts in the epidermis, which is mostly made up of squamous cells.

Like basal cell carcinoma, this type of skin cancer is highly treatable. However, squamous cell carcinoma is more aggressive than basal cell carcinoma. That means that squamous cell carcinoma spreads faster.

This type of cancer usually appears as bumps or red scaly patches of skin on the face, ears, lips and mouth. Squamous cell carcinoma can spread to other parts of the body and can grow into large areas.

Malignant Melanoma

This kind of cancer is the most deadly, and accounts for about 75 percent of skin cancer deaths. According to the American Cancer Society, melanoma accounted for about 62,190 cases of skin cancer in 2006 and most—about 7,910—of the 10,710 deaths due to skin cancer each year.

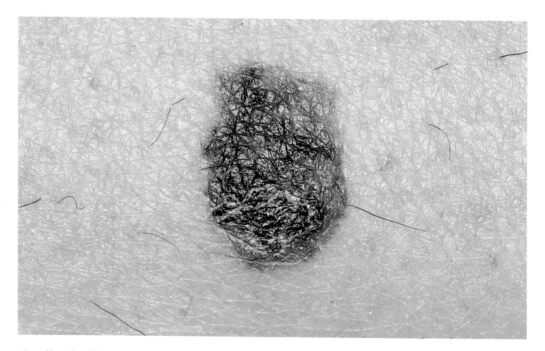

Usually, the first symptom of malignant melanoma is having irregularly shaped moles on the skin. If it is caught early, malignant melanoma can be treated to prevent serious complications.

Pediatric Melanoma

Each year, pediatric melanoma—the type of melanoma that children develop—affects only seven children out of one million, or about five hundred children. That number is on the rise. According to the Skin Cancer Foundation, there has been more than a 100 percent increase in the cases of pediatric melanoma in the past twenty years.

Malignant melanoma is skin cancer that is quick to spread. ("Malignant" refers to something that grows uncontrollably and is dangerous to a person's health.) Malignant melanoma starts in the melanocytes as moles that change and become cancerous. This type of cancer appears most often in fair-skinned men and women. But people with all types of skin can be at risk. Early detection is important since melanoma is almost 100 percent curable if is it found early. Left untreated or undetected, malignant melanoma can spread to other organs in the body, possibly causing death.

Actinic Keratosis

Basal cell carcinoma accounts for about 80 percent of all skin
In addition to the skin changes caused by the three main
types of skin cancer, there is another warning sign that cells
in the skin are changing. Actinic keratosis (AK)—also known
as a solar keratosis—is a small crusty, scaly, or crumbly bump
on the skin surface. AK can be hard to spot because it may
be light or dark, tan, pink, red, or a combination of these. AK
can even be same color as the skin. The scale or crust is dry
and rough, and is often found through touch, rather by sight.
Sometimes the area itches or is tender when it is touched.
Skin affected by AK can also become swollen and surrounded
by redness. In rare instances, actinic keratoses can bleed.

The AK lesion develops slowly and usually grows to be
about an eighth to a quarter of an inch in length. Sometimes
the lesion can be as large as one inch. Early on, it may disappear only to reappear later. It is not unusual to spot several patches of AK at one time. AK is most likely to appear on
the face, lips, ears, scalp, neck, backs of the hands and fore-
arms, shoulders, and back. These are all parts of the body
most often exposed to sunlight.

Actinic keratosis is dangerous because it can be the first
step to developing skin cancer. If treated early, almost all AK
spots can be eliminated without becoming skin cancers. But
left untreated, around 10 percent may progress to squamous
cell carcinoma. Although squamous cell cancers are usually

not life-threatening when detected and treated in the early stages, they can still grow large and invade the surrounding tissues. Sometimes they can also spread to and damage internal organs. Another form of AK, actinic cheilitis, develops on the lips and may evolve into a type of squamous cell skin cancer that can spread rapidly to other parts of the body.

According to the Skin Cancer Foundation, ongoing and unprotected exposure to the Sun is the cause of almost all AK. Sun damage to the skin builds up over time, so that even brief exposure adds to the lifetime total of sun damage. The likelihood of developing AK is highest in regions near the equator. AK spots can also appear on skin that has been frequently exposed to artificial sources of ultraviolet light, such as tanning beds or other devices used in tanning salons. More rarely, they may be caused by long-term exposure to X rays or some industrial chemicals. Older people are more likely than younger ones to develop AK, because Sun exposure builds up over the years. Some experts believe that the majority of people who live to the age of eighty will have spots of AK. However, a lot of a person's lifetime Sun exposure occurs before age twenty. As a result, AK also appears in people in their early twenties who have spent too much time in the Sun with little or no protection.

WHAT CAUSES SKIN CANCER

Nearly 90 percent of all skin cancers are believed to come

from exposure to the Sun's ultraviolet (UV) rays. There are several different kinds of UV rays coming from the Sun. The two types associated with skin cancer are UVA and UVB. UVA stands for ultraviolet-A. These are the long-wave solar rays that penetrate the skin more deeply. They are considered to be the chief cause of skin wrinkling and "leathering." UVB stands for ultraviolet-B. These short-wave solar rays are more likely than UVA rays to produce sunburn. These rays are considered the main cause of basal and squamous cell carcinomas, and are also a significant cause of melanoma. The latest studies show that UVA not only increases UVB's cancer-causing effects, but may directly cause some skin cancers, including melanomas.

Ozone Dangers

Some UV rays are not able to reach the Earth's surface thanks to the Earth's ozone layer. This is a layer of atmosphere that filters out many of the damaging UV rays. However, the overall level of UV light reaching the Earth's surface is increasing because our planet's atmospheric ozone layer is thinning over certain parts of the globe. According to the Skin Cancer Foundation, "The greatest hazard humans face from the effects of ozone depletion is skin cancer."

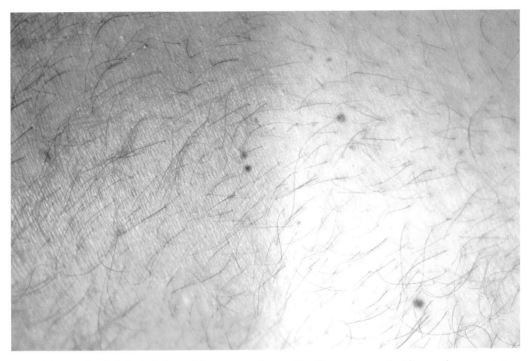

The skin on the left is bright red from a sunburn. Healthy unburned skin can be seen on the right.

Prolonged or frequent exposure to the Sun can cause sunburns on the skin. Sunburned skin is damaged and turns red and painful. Serious sunburns result in skin blisters. Eventually the burned skin will dry out and become crusty or flaky and may peel off. Besides the sunburn symptoms you can see on your skin, the Sun's rays are also damaging your skin cells on skin layers you cannot see. Studies show that even one sunburn that produces blisters on the skin more than doubles a person's chance of developing melanoma later in life. A history of three or more sunburns—especially

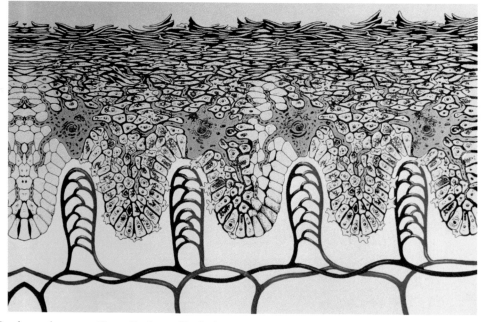

Sunburn damages the cells in mulitple layers of skin, not just the top layer. This kind of damage can lead to skin cancer.

blistering sunburns—before age twenty, greatly increases the risk of developing skin cancer.

Research has also shown that there are other risk factors for developing skin cancer. These include having a family history of skin cancer, having a fair-skinned complexion, or having moles that have been present since birth.

Family History
Researchers have found that the risk of melanoma is more than two times higher in people who have a close relative

with skin cancer. While having a family member with skin cancer does not automatically mean that all other family members will get skin cancer, it does mean that everyone in the family should be aware of the risks.

Chemical Exposure

Your skin is being exposed to chemicals constantly—in the soaps and lotions you use, in the air around you, and on the things you touch. You cannot avoid coming into contact with some kinds of chemicals. Most of these everyday chemicals are usually harmless in small amounts. (The chemicals in soaps and other skin products have been tested to make sure they are safe.)

Some chemicals, however, cause changes in your cells when they come into contact with your skin. Insecticides, which are chemicals used to kill insects, often contain substances that are dangerous. Arsenic is often present in insecticides (and in some water supplies) and can increase your risk of developing nonmelanoma skin cancer. People who work in factories with chemicals and other industrial materials are also at a higher risk of developing some types of skin cancer.

Smoking

Smoking tobacco found in cigarettes, cigars, and pipes may also cause skin cancer or at least increase the risk of developing

The Dangers of Tanning Beds

For many years people thought that tanning salons were a safe alternative to natural Sun or a way to prevent sunburn. This is because tanning machines were said to produce only UVA rays and not UVB rays, which are responsible for most sunburns. Researchers have since learned that tanning beds do produce UVB rays. They have also learned that UVA light is not as safe as once thought. Even though UVA is less likely to cause sunburn, it can still cause long-term damage to the skin. The UV rays from artificial sources of light, such as tanning beds and Sun lamps, are just as dangerous as those from the Sun. An unprotected "fake bake"—lying in a tanning bed without the proper sunscreen—is not safer than a day at the beach without sunscreen.

As for using tanning beds to prevent sunburn before a vacation or to get a safe "base tan," this is also false. A visit to a tanning bed, followed by natural Sun exposure can cause—not prevent—sunburn.

The only kind of tan that does not include UV rays involves special self-tanning chemicals. Most of these lotions or sprays have a substance called dihydroxyacetone (DHA), which colors the skin. However, these are not 100 percent safe, since some people can develop allergic skin reactions to the chemicals.

skin cancer. Scientists already know that smoking is linked to other types of cancer, such as mouth and lung cancers. The chemicals that enter the body when you inhale tobacco smoke kill and damage healthy cells. Damaged cells can become cancerous and spread to different parts of the body.

Radiation Exposure

In some cases, people are intentionally exposed to radiation. Radiation therapy is used to treat certain kinds of cancers. Research has shown that targeted radiation can kill some cancer cells. Unfortunately, the radiation therapy that some children undergo for cancer treatments may increase their risks of developing a nonmelanoma skin cancer.

Skin Conditions

Certain skin conditions can increase a person's risk of developing skin cancer. Sometimes serious injuries to the skin can raise the chances for nonmelanoma skin cancer. Most people have scars on their skin where an injury or wound healed. Scars are made up of tissue and other cells that join together to repair or cover parts of the skin that have been injured. In rare cases, nonmelanoma skin cancers grow in scars that come from very bad burns.

Psoriasis is a skin condition that is non-cancerous and is not contagious. People with psoriasis have skin that may become inflamed (irritated) or may appear scaly. Treatment

3

THE HISTORY OF SKIN CANCER

Although new ways of detecting and treating cancer are discovered every day, the disease has been around for at least as long as the earliest medical records were kept. The earliest known descriptions of cancer were written on papyrus, an early form of paper made from the papyrus plant. These papyri were discovered and translated in the nineteenth century and provided the first real knowledge of Egyptian medicine. Two of the documents, called the Edwin Smith and George Ebers papyri, contain descriptions of cancer that were written around 1600 BCE These documents used sources from as early as 2500 BCE. The Smith papyrus describes surgery, while the Ebers papyrus outlines medications and other forms of treatments that could today be classified as "magic."

By studying these papyri, scholars believe that Egyptians were able to tell the difference between **benign** tumors, or tumors that are non-cancerous, and malignant tumors. The papyri also show that ancient Egyptians did not believe that cancer could be cured. They felt that cancer could only be treated by destroying the tissues of the body that were affected by the cancer. Most often, the cancer would be removed through surgery or through something called the fire drill. This tool was used to burn the tumor in order to kill the cancerous cells. At this point, scholars did not know what caused cancer, they only knew that it had to be removed.

EARLY THEORIES

Early cultures believed that cancer and other illness was caused by the gods. If you angered the gods or did something wrong, you would be struck with an illness as a form of punishment.

About a thousand years later, medical and scientific research began to explore physical causes of illnesses like cancer. The word "cancer" came from Hippocrates. He was a well known doctor who lived in ancient Greece sometime between 460 and 370 BCE. He is commonly called the Father of Medicine. Hippocrates began calling the cancerous tumors *karkinos,* which is the Greek word for "crab." Hippocrates thought the tumors looked like crabs.

Hippocrates also believed that the body was composed of four fluids: blood, phlegm, yellow bile, and black bile. He believed that too much black bile in any given site of the body was the cause of cancer. This theory was accepted for about a thousand years before it was proven to be incorrect. (There is no such thing as black bile.) As the ancient teachings of Hippocrates were translated, his research spread throughout Europe. This work continued to inspire physicians for thousands of years.

There were other theories about the cause of different types of cancer. Some had some inkling of truth, but others were completely wrong. In some cases, it would take hundreds of years before the incorrect theories were disproved.

Though they may have been proved wrong, early theories and beliefs helped doctors and scientists learn more about the human body and how it works.

Lymph Theory

Among the theories that replaced Hippocrates's bile theory was the idea that cancer was caused by fluid called lymph. In the 1600s an Italian physician named Gaspare Aselli discovered the vessels of the lymphatic system. The lymphatic system is a system of thin tubes that runs throughout the body. Tubes called lymph vessels branch through all parts of the body like the arteries and veins that carry blood. However, the lymphatic system was responsible for circulating a colorless liquid called lymph. Aselli believed that cancer developed as lymph was moved from the blood into the body. Later scientists, such as John Hunter—who lived in the 1700s—also believed that lymph could cause cancer.

Today, researchers know that the lymphatic system is an important part of the immune system. Lymph helps move immune cells that fight diseases and other illnesses. Aselli and other scientists were partially correct in their theories. Lymph can spread cancerous cells to other parts of the body. But scientists today know that lymph is not the main reason why cells become cancerous.

Blastema Theory

In the 1830s, German scientist Johannes Muller disagreed that cancer came from lymph. Instead, he believed that cancer was made up of cells. Specifically, he believed that cancer came from blastema. Blastema is a grouping of cellular material that usually develops into an organ or body part.

One of his students, Rudolph Virchow, proved Muller's theory to be incorrect. Virchow's research showed that cancer cells developed from other cells, not from blastema. Some of the things that Virchow was

Rudolph Virchow's many discoveries helped pave the way for modern medicine.

famous for included proving that all cells came from other similar cells and finding ways to spot certain types of cancers. Virchow is also credited as being one of the first scientists to recognize leukemia, a blood disease that is often considered a type of blood cancer.

Chronic Irritation and Trauma

Virchow believed that cancer could be caused by chronic or long-lasting irritation. According to Virchow, the cancer then spread to the rest of the body "like a liquid." This liquid theory was proven wrong when Karl Thiersch's research showed that cancer spreads throughout the body when malignant cells multiply.

Similar to the chronic irritation theory, many scientists during the 1800s believed that cancer could be caused by trauma or an injury to part of the body. In the 1920s this theory was proven wrong. Today, scientists agree that trauma or an injury cannot cause most cancers. There are, however, exceptions, such as severe scarring or serious skin burns leading to skin cancer.

Parasites

Parasites are organisms that live inside or on a host organism. The host organism supplies the parasites with food, nutrients, and a place to live. Unfortunately, the parasite usually makes the host sick or kills the host. Examples of parasites include, ticks, fleas, and some types of worm. Since the 1700s cancer was often blamed on parasites like worms. This theory was so widespread that in 1926 a Nobel Prize was awarded for research that said that a specific worm caused stomach cancer. However, scientists cannot prove that parasites cause cancer, so this theory is considered false.

ADVANCES IN CANCER RESEARCH

Part of the reason why some cancer theories were proven wrong has to do with improved technology. In the late

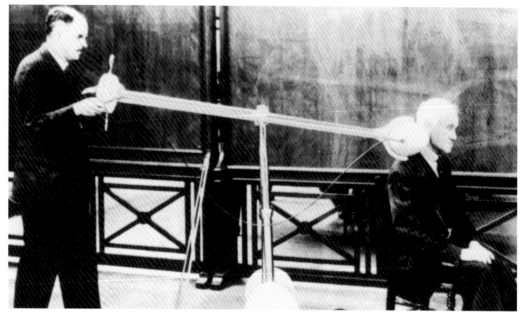

Early forms of cancer treatment included shining radioactive lights on cancerous spots. New technologies and health discoveries helped to improve cancer treatment.

nineteenth century, the creation of better microscopes made it possible for physicians to examine cells and their activities more closely. By studying cancer tissues and tumors under powerful microscopes, doctors could tell that cancer cells did not look like the normal cells surrounding the tissues. Researchers then began to focus on how the disease changes the cells.

In the twentieth century, cancer research grew into a branch of science called **oncology**, which focuses on the causes and treatment of cancer. Two important events in 1913 helped the public better understand cancer. One event was the first known article on cancer's warning signs being published in a popular magazine for women. Also, the American Cancer Society was established as the first nation-wide organization dedicated to public education on cancer.

As public awareness of cancer grew, many organizations were formed to conduct their own research and to help fund research for other institutions. In 1937, the United States Congress passed the national Cancer Institute Act. The Act created the National Cancer Institute, which is still active today. The American Cancer Society also continues to search for new ways to diagnose and treat cancer. To date, the Society's research program has invested about $3 billion in cancer research.

In 1971, President Richard M. Nixon signed the National Cancer Act, which launched a national Cancer Program administered by the National Cancer Institute. Since that time, biomedical research supported by the National Cancer Institute has advanced the understanding of cancer in the United States.

However, the war against cancer is being fought in many countries. For example, the National Cancer Institute funded activities run by the University of Florida-College of Nursing's Worldwide Cancer Prevention and Control program. Started in the 1990s, this program ran for fifteen years. It was designed to increase the number of nurses who would be prepared to address issues of cancer prevention and control in other countries. Through the years, more than one hundred nurses from seventy-seven different countries attended these learning workshops. Though the workshops have ended, the program has created workbooks that will help with cancer prevention in other countries.

Elsewhere in the world, the World Health Organization (WHO) continues the fight against cancer. The World Health Organization is the United Nations' agency for health.

THE WAR ON SKIN CANCER

Though skin cancer has probably been around as long as most other cancers, scientists and doctors were not able to diagnose it until technology improved. Without powerful microscopes they could not see the changes happening to the skin on a cellular level. Additionally, until scientists learned more about the Sun and its rays, they did not know that UV rays could cause skin cancer.

Fortunately, science has progressed enough so that many different causes and types of skin cancer have been identified. Armed with knowledge on prevention and treatment, many organizations are working together to inform and help the public. For example, a global UV project called INTERSUN involves many groups, including WHO, the United Nations Environment Program, the World Meteorological Organization, and the International Agency on Cancer Research and

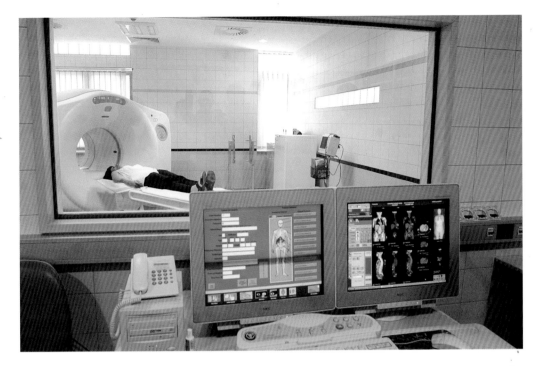

New scanning technologies can help doctors identify cancer in different parts of the body. Early detection can lead to more successful treatments.

International Commission on Non-Ionizing Radiation Protection. Together, these organizations fight skin cancer by measuring the health risks that lead to skin cancer. They then put together guidelines, recommendations, and information that can help people understand how to protect themselves against skin cancer.

INTERSUN also provides guidance to national authorities and other agencies about effective Sun awareness programs. These programs address different audiences, such as people exposed to skin cancer through their jobs, tourists, school children, and the general public. For example, in 2003 WHO

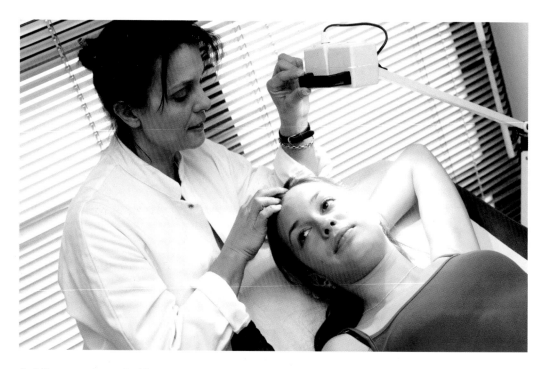

Public awareness of skin cancer and its causes has helped many people. Knowing that they are at risk allows them to talk to their doctors to make sure that any suspicious skin conditions are carefully checked.

published a brochure called *Artificial Tanning Beds: Risks and Guidance* providing advice on how using tanning beds affects public health.

In addition to these groups, individual physicians, scientists, and researchers worldwide are also making exciting discoveries about how **genes** play a role in causing cancer. Genes are tiny parts of cells that determine characteristics and traits. For example, some genes can decide if you have blue eyes or brown hair. Genes are passed down from parent to child.

Scientists think that higher risks of cancer in families can be attributed to genes that are common in families. Since some research has shown that 10 percent of people with melanoma have relatives with melanoma, scientists believe that there must e a hereditary or genetic link. Some scientists have even identified a specific gene that has mutated, or changed, in people who have malignant melanoma. Genetic studies are still ongoing. Many hope that understanding the connection between genes and diseases will help with treatment or a cure.

Research into genetics and heredity may someday provide a cure for skin cancer and other diseases.

4

DIAGNOSING AND TREATING SKIN CANCER

Being diagnosed with skin cancer can be scary. But nearly everyone diagnosed with skin cancer can undergo procedures that will help to treat it. The first step is finding out whether a skin mark is cancerous, or if it is simply one of the normal and harmless spots that most people have on their bodies.

DIAGNOSIS

Fortunately, skin cancer does not develop overnight. In particular, moles that develop into melanoma go through a series of changes known as **dysplasia,** or a period during which cells experience abnormal growth. A mole is more likely to turn into a melanoma if the growth is very abnormal.

This series of changes is easy to detect. The problem is that most people either do not know to look for these changes or ignore the changes. According to the Melanoma

Research Foundation, every hour of every day of the year, an American dies of malignant melanoma. This is especially tragic since melanoma can often be prevented and, when it does occur, can be treated if it is spotted early. To detect melanoma, doctors recommend that people learn the five signs that may indicate that skin cancer is developing.

These five signs are commonly known as the ABCDE's of skin cancer:

A stands for **a**symmetry. Normal moles or freckles are symmetrical. That means that if an imaginary line were drawn down the center of the mole, the two halves would be mirror images of each other. In cases of skin cancer, spots will not look the same on both sides.

B stands for **b**order. A mole or spot with blurry or jagged edges may be precancerous.

C stands for **c**olor. A person should check if a mole is a single color or if it is darker in some parts. A doctor should examine any mole that is more than one color. Normal skin spots are usually one color. Moles that change in color should also be examined by a doctor. Changes in color can include lightening or darkening of the mole.

D stands for **d**iameter. If the mole is larger than a pencil eraser—about one-sixth of an inch—it needs to be examined by a doctor. This includes areas that do not have any other abnormalities, such as color, border, or asymmetry.

E stands for **e**levation. A mole that is elevated or raised above the rest of the skin should be examined.

Other warning signs of skin cancer include a mole that grows very fast, forms a sore, itches, or bleeds.

While these are excellent ways to determine whether or not a mole is cancerous, it is important to remember that having these signs or symptoms does not automatically mean that a mole is cancerous. But they are definitely reasons to speak to a dermatologist in order to get an expert's opinion.

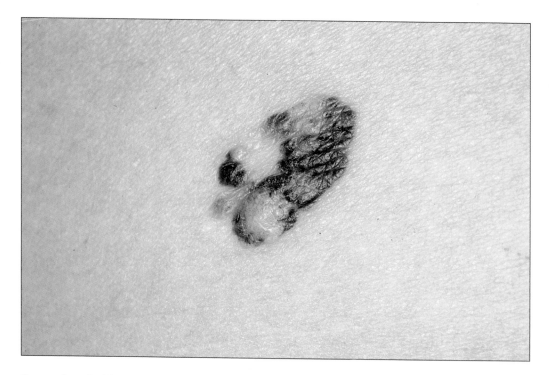

Do not be afraid to tell your doctor about any skin growths or marks that look strange.

During a biopsy, a skin sample is collected and sent to a laboratory for testing.

If the dermatologist suspects that a mole, spot, freckle, or other kind of skin lesion might be cancerous, the doctor will order a **biopsy.** A biopsy is a test that can help doctors tell whether a spot on the skin is cancerous, or is benign, or harmless. The physician performing the procedure will explain the reason for the biopsy, the type of biopsy to be performed, and how the procedure will be performed.

The biopsy is usually performed in a dermatologist's office or in an outpatient setting, which means that the procedure takes place in a hospital but the patient does not need to stay there overnight. Before the procedure, the patient is given medication—usually an injection—that will numb the area around the skin that is being removed.

Depending upon the size and location of the suspected skin cancer, different types of biopsies may be performed. An excisional biopsy removes the suspicious area, including some healthy skin. This kind of biopsy is used if the abnormal mole or growth is small in size. If the suspicious area is very large, an incisional biopsy may be performed. This involves removing only a small part of the area. Depending upon how much skin is removed, healing times for these biopsies can vary.

A needle biopsy is used when looking for cancer in tissues beneath the skin or in organs inside the body. (Cancer found in those places might have spread from some types of skin cancer.) A hollow needle is inserted into the tissue or organ in order to remove a sample of cells. Doctors performing needle biopsies often use X ray or other forms of scans or imaging to help them place the needle in the correct area.

The samples taken during a biopsy are sent to a special laboratory. The technicians there will examine the cells to see if cancer is present. The laboratory can also determine what kind of cancer a person has. If the results are not definite, more samples may be needed.

The dermatologist receives the results from the laboratory and explains them to the patient. If cancer is present, the dermatologist may discuss treatment options with the patient. In some cases, a dermatologist will send the patient to see an oncologist, or a doctor who specializes in cancer.

TREATMENT

Most types of skin cancer are treated through surgery. Different types of surgery include cryosurgery (destruction by freezing), laser surgery (using a laser beam to cut away or vaporize growths), and a method that use a spoon-like blade to scoop out the growth, followed by destruction of surrounding tissue with an electric needle. Occasionally, other treatments such as radiation therapy or **chemotherapy** may be used alone or in combination to kill cancer cells.

Physicians also use a technique called Mohs' surgery, which is named after its inventor Dr. Frederic Mohs. The operation usually takes place under local

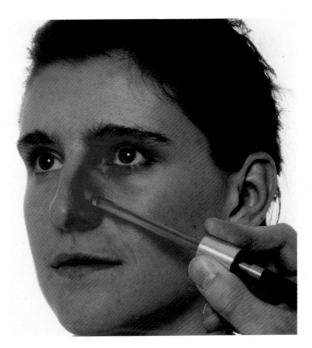

This form of skin cancer treatment uses special creams and high-powered lamps to kill cancer cells.

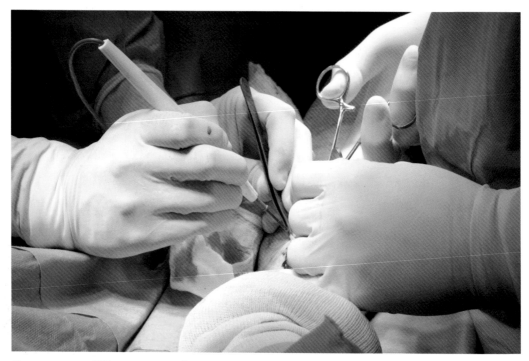

Surgeons use different types of surgery to remove cancerous tissue.

anesthesia, meaning that only the area being operated on is numbed and the patient is awake. Usually, the surgery does not require an overnight stay in the hospital. Patients are treated on an outpatient basis, either in the doctor's office or in a hospital room, and return home the same day. Physicians performing Mohs' surgery carefully shave away slices of cancerous skin, one layer at a time. As each layer is removed, it is checked under the microscope to see if any abnormal cells are on the edges of the removed tissue. This process is continued until no abnormal cells are seen.

Mohs' surgery tries to remove all of the cancer cells, while saving as much healthy tissue as possible. This also reducing the amount of scarring left behind after the surgery. This technique is used most often to remove cancerous areas that do not have a clear starting and ending point. It is also used to remove lesions on parts of the body—such as the nose, lips, ears, or eyelids—where it is important to remove the least amount of healthy skin possible. Mohs' surgery is used

What If the Cancer Spreads?

Cancerous cells can spread throughout the body, affecting a number of different organs and body systems. When this happens, it is called metastasis. Treatment options depend upon the type of cancer and how badly it has spread. Doctors will try to remove as much cancer as possible from affected organs. This is usually done through surgery. Chemotherapy and radiation are often used in addition to surgery. In some cases, a person can recover if the metastasis is not widespread. However, if the cancerous cells in the body are too numerous, or vital organs or systems have been affected by the cancer, surgery or other treatments may not be helpful. This level of metastasis often results in death. This is why it is important to try to catch cancerous growths before they spread.

most often for squamous and basal cell cancers and, more recently, for some melanomas. Depending on the amount of cancerous cells removed, Mohs' surgery may be followed by surgery to cover scars or to return the area to a more normal appearance.

AFTER TREATMENT

After undergoing treatment for skin cancer, many people have questions about the disease and its aftereffects. Some might ask if a scare will go away or fade, or how to keep the cancer from coming back.

Basic follow-up care usually involves keeping the incision clean and bandaged for a short time, using sunblock every time a person goes outsides, conducting monthly self-exams, and going to the doctor to be examined. For most people, a scar will fade over time.

About 5 percent of patients will develop a second melanoma in their lifetime, while others may develop more growth from the original tumor. Because skin cancer has a tendency to show up again and again once it is found, all patients require follow-up care. Patients should be evaluated every three to six months for three years. After that, they should be examined every six to twelve months for two years. Eventually, if the doctor feels confident that the cancer is not spreading, the patient may be checked out only once a year.

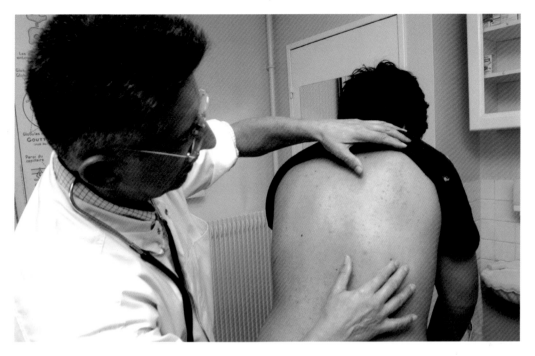

Regular skin check-ups are a must for anyone who has been treated for skin cancer.

Different scans or imaging techniques may also be used to check for cancerous growths. These tests can help a doctor spot cancer that he or she would not see from the outside.

PREVENTION

It is a good idea for everyone—especially people who are more likely to develop skin cancer—to talk to their doctors about skin care. A "skin check" can be a part of regular medical care. This will help your doctor look out for skin cancer and can also help you learn more about skin cancer prevention.

By far, the best way to avoid developing skin cancer or preventing it from reoccurring is to follow "safe Sun" practices. Of course, it is nearly impossible to spend all hours indoors. Getting

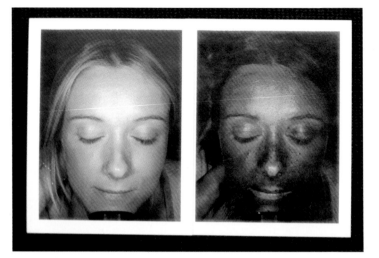

Sun damage to your skin builds up over your lifetime. The photo on the left shows a person's face under normal light. Special lighting used on the right shows how much Sun damage is beneath the top layers of skin.

no Sun exposure can be dangerous. Your body needs some sunlight to function properly. But there is no need to hide from the Sun completely or wrap up like a mummy before heading out the door. Following a few safety guidelines can help you protect your skin from harmful UV rays that may cause cancer. It is especially important to follow these guidelines when spending time outdoors between 10:00 a.m. and 4:00 p.m. This is when the Sun's rays are strongest.

Sunscreen and Sunblock

It is important to wear sunscreen or sunblock all year and not just in the summertime. You can get sunburn participating in winter sports, such as skiing or sledding. Besides

Slip! Slop! Slap!

Beginning in 2006, the American Cancer Society designated the month of May as Skin Cancer Awareness Month. Programs by the society—and other cancer organizations—encourage people to learn more about skin cancer and how to prevent it.

The American Cancer Society has also developed Sun safety guidelines they call Slip! Slop! Slap!:

Slip! On a Shirt. Protect skin with clothing.

Slop! On Sunscreen. Use a sunscreen with a Sun protection factor (SPF) of 15 or higher.

Slap! On a Hat Wear a hat with a wide brim. A person's ears, neck, and face get a lot of Sun.

getting hit directly by the rays from the Sun, the snow or ice can also reflect the rays onto your skin. Even when it is cloudy outside, you should use some kind of skin protection. Clouds do not cut down the UV rays. In fact, clouds may actually reflect the UV rays, making them stronger and more dangerous to the skin.

When buying sunblock or sunscreen, read the labels carefully. You should purchase a product with an SPF (Sun

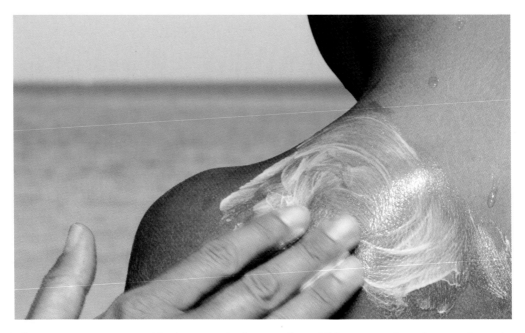

It is important to use sunblock on any body part that will be exposed to the sun. Reapply the lotion often if you are swimming, sweating, or using insect repellent.

Protection Factor) of at least 15 for daily wear. Use a product with an SPF of 30 or higher when you will be outdoors for long periods of time. The SPF number tells how much longer people can stay in the Sun without getting sunburned. So, if someone normally burns after 20 minutes and they put on a sunscreen with an SPF rating of 15, this sunscreen will give them 15 times the protection. That is 15 times 20 minutes, or 300 minutes (5 hours). The sunscreen label should also say that it offers both UVA and UVB protection. This is called broad spectrum protection, and will ensure that you will be protected from the different types of the Sun's UV rays.

Try to stay away from products containing the chemical PABA, since some people could have an allergic reaction to it. In addition, look for sunblocks that contain titanium dioxide or zinc oxide. Zinc oxide has been shown to block both UVA and UVB rays. Check to make sure that these ingredients are listed in the active ingredients section of the label.

Be sure to put the lotion on all exposed parts of your body, not just on your arms and legs. Use it on the tops of your ears, the back of the neck, on the face, and the tops of the feet. Have your parent apply the lotion to your back or to other hard-to-reach places. Reapply the sunscreen or sunblock every two to three hours. This should be done more often if you are sweating or swimming—even if the lotion is waterproof. It is easier to get sunburned when swimming or boating because the reflection from the water intensifies the Sun's rays. You should also remember that some sunscreens are waterproof, but no sunscreens are towel-proof! Reapply sunscreen every time its gets wiped off with a towel after swimming or sweating.

Other Forms of Sun Protection

Wearing a hat is a good way to protect your face and your ears from UV rays. The hats that offer the best protection, have long or wide brims. Hats with brims that surround the entire head—including the back of the neck—work well.

Summertime is not the only time to use Sun protection. In the winter, the Sun's rays are very strong when they reflect off of the snow. When playing outdoors, skiing, or snow-boarding, you should use proper eye protection and sunblock on your face.

Many people use baseball caps to block the Sun. This provides some protection for your face, but it also leaves your ears and neck exposed to harmful rays.

Your eyes can also be damaged by UVA and UVB rays. (This is one reason why you should never look directly into the Sun.) Melanoma can form when the backs of the eyes are damaged by harmful rays. Using sunglasses when you are outdoors on a sunny day can help. Look for sunglasses with a UVA/UVB label. This label means that the lenses are coated to protect eyes from harmful rays. Larger-framed glasses provide the best protection.

Do not count on the windows and automobile windshields for protection unless they have been specially treated. Research has shown that UV rays can come through car windows and windshields and damage a person's skin. According to some studies, more than a third of Americans are spending more time in their cars than in previous years. On average, people are spending more than fifteen hours per week on the road, or about thirty-two days a year! It is important to remember to protect your skin, even when you are inside a car.

Some medications and vitamin or mineral supplements can affect your skin, making you more likely to get a sunburn. Your doctor or pharmacist can warn you about these side effects so that you can take proper Sun precautions.

THE FUTURE OF SKIN CANCER

Someday, scientists hope to find a cure for cancer. Until then, physicians recommend that patients avoid cancer-causing behavior. Do not smoke. Eat healthy foods. Exercise regularly for overall health. Be safe in the Sun. The best way to deal with cancer is to do anything possible to prevent it.

GLOSSARY

benign—Not harmful.

biopsy—A procedure that involves removing body tissue in order to examine cells for cancer or other diseases.

chemotherapy—Cancer treatment that involves using chemicals to kill cancerous cells.

dermatologist—A doctor who specializes in the skin and its diseases or disorders.

dermis—The second layer of skin.

diagnose—To identify an illness or disease.

dysplasia—A period during which cells experience abnormal growth.

epidermis—The outermost layer of skin.

genes—Tiny parts of cells that determine characteristics and traits.

immune system—The body system responsible for fighting off illness and disease.

integumentary system—Another name for the skin.

melanin—Substance in the skin that gives the skin color and protects it from harmful ultraviolet Sun rays.

melanocytes—Skin cells that produce melanin. Damaged or irregular melanocytes can develop into skin cancer.

melanoma—A type of cancer that starts in the melanocytes. Melanomas are the most deadly forms of skin cancer.

oncology—The branch of medicine that deals with cancer.

subcutis—The innermost layer of skin.

sunblock—A type of lotion used on the skin to block the Sun's harmful ultraviolet rays.

sunscreen—A type of lotion used on the skin that filters some of the Sun's harmful ultraviolet rays. Sunscreen can also block some of the Sun's rays.

ultraviolet (UV) rays—Invisible rays from the Sun. These rays can cause changes in the skin that may lead to skin cancer.

FIND OUT MORE

Books

Gregson, Susan R. Skin Care. Mankato, MN: LifeMatters, 2000.

Egan, Tracie. *Skin Cancer: Current and Emerging Trends in Detection and Treatment.* New York: The Rosen Publishing Group, 2006.

Simons, Rae. *For All to See: a Teen's Guide to Healthy Skin.* Broomall, PA: Mason Crest Publishers, 2005.

Hall, Margaret. *Skin Deep.* Chicago: Raintree, 2006.

Web Sites

KidsHealth: How to Be Safe When You're in the Sun
http://www.kidshealth.org/kid/watch/out/summer_safety.html

KidsHealth: The Whole Story on Skin
http://www.kidshealth.org/kid/body/skin_noSW.html

The Skin Cancer Foundation: SunSmart Parents and Kids
http://www.skincancer.org/children/index.php

Sun Safety for Kids
http://www.sunsafetyforkids.org/

INDEX

Page numbers for illustrations are in **boldface**